Di Halliday

# A Word
## For All Seasons

*Reflections, Meditations and Prayers for the Church Year*

**Mary Hathaway**

First published in 1997 by
KEVIN MAYHEW LTD
Rattlesden
Bury St Edmunds
Suffolk IP30 0SZ



0 1 2 3 4 5 6 7 8 9

ISBN 1 84003 018 6
Catalogue 1500122

Cover photograph courtesy of Images Colour Library Limited

Cover design by Jaquetta Sergeant
Edited by Janet Payne
Typesetting by Louise Hill
Printed and bound in Great Britain.

# Contents

# Introduction

It never ceases to amaze me how relevant the Bible is to our everyday life. The problems and joys people in the Bible faced are so similar to our own. Each piece in this original collection is rooted in my everyday experience, as I have made my spiritual journey through many years. The events that give rise to the festivals of the Church involve interaction between God and ordinary people. So it was natural that many pieces fit into the framework of the Church year, beginning with Advent and ending with All Saints, although some could be used at any time.

There are reflections, meditations, prayers and insights. They can be used in a variety of situations: public worship, house groups and other small gatherings, also privately by individuals. Some lend themselves to the use of more than one voice, and could be presented dramatically. Others are set out to be used responsively by a worship leader and congregation.

It was said of Jesus that people wondered at the beautiful words he spoke. He also managed to communicate truth at many levels at the same time. Children enjoyed his stories and yet the theologians of his day wrestled with the depths of meaning in what Jesus said, even though they were listening to the same words. So if we sit at Jesus' feet and learn of him, words used in worship can be understandable in different ways to different people and be beautiful as well.

Many people today have little or no Church background and yet may well attend a Service or some sort of religious event at major Church Festivals such as Christmas or Easter. So this collection takes into account not only Church members but those on the fringes of the Church and those who may be outside it altogether. So wherever people are on their own spiritual journey, or whether they are aware of being on a spiritual journey at all, I pray that there will be something in this book which will speak to them of Jesus.

Mary Hathaway

# Advent

## *Light in darkness*

*Leader* Beautiful is the moonrise
in a circle of perfection,
her face is pale gold
and the light she spreads
is silver.

*All* But more beautiful
is the mind of our God
who brought light
out of darkness
before time began.

*Leader* Lovely are the stars
as they sprinkle
the heavens
with gladness.

*All* But more lovely
is the joy of our God
for his laughter
fills the universe.

*Leader* Deep are the shadows
of the moonlight lying
in pools of blackness.

*All* But deeper are the ways
of our God and his thoughts
beyond our knowing.

*Leader* How lovely is light
when it shines
in darkness!

*All* But how terrible is night
without moonlight
and how lonely the sky
without stars!

*Leader* But the Lord our God
who created all things
says to his children,
'Do not fear.'

*All* 'For you have
the moon at night
and the sun by day
but me you have always
to light your path.'

# *Morning star of God*

*Leader* Morning star of God,
rising in beauty from
the ashes of our night,
encourage us your servants
who walk in darkness
and need the loving
touch of your light
to lift us into joy.

*All* Be gracious to us
for without your light
we are left in our
darkness for ever.

*Leader* Morning star of God,
clothed in unattainable glory,
enfold us in your
robes of light,
that we may stand
in gladness before you
in the beauty
of your presence.

*All* Be gracious to us
for without your light
we are left in our
darkness for ever.

*Leader* Morning star of God,
our joy and our desiring,
come to us we beseech you,
shine upon us once again
for life is cold without you.
Our bodies, minds and spirits
ache with longing for
the glory of your light.

*All* Be gracious to us
for without your light
we are left in our
darkness for ever.

# *Journey to the heart of Christmas*

I owe my children so much.
They have taught me
  many things about you.
But I cannot give them
  my experience of Christmas,
  they must find their own.
As the shepherds had only
  a short journey
  to the manger
  but the wise men
  travelled many months
  to find the same stable,
  so only you know
  whether theirs will be
  a long or a short journey.

So does it matter then
  that all the preparations
  seem to leave me so little
  time to find you?
For these outward things
  are signposts of love
  that I can leave to guide
  them on their journey.
For I cannot go with them
  to the heart of Christmas.
No one finds you there
  unless they travel alone.

But now it is my turn
  to stand aside
  and make room for them
  to go beyond me.
And as I watch them go,
  I pray for them,
  that they may come through
  the outward layer
  of noise and razzmatazz,
  to find the place
  of peace and stillness,
  where they too
  can see the star
  and hear the angels singing.

# *The secret*

I carry a secret,
  a wonderful secret,
  it lives and moves and stirs in me.
We created a person,
  a new human being,
  it grows in my body so silently.

Christ grew in secret,
  the world's greatest secret,
  part of his mother hidden inside.
Then born as a baby,
  a perfect little baby,
  helpless, dependent, he fed and cried.

But while still in the womb
  this tiny baby's fingers
  reached out in love and touched every land.
He was creation,
  not just one of its creatures,
  and he held the world in his unborn hand.

# Christmas

## *Flame of love*

*Leader* Lord Jesus Christ,
come and be seen in us
for the world needs your light.
We are but poor lanterns
but we are open to you.

Come and be seen in us
*All* for the world needs your light.

*Leader* Lord Jesus Christ,
be born yet again
this Christmas
in the empty spaces of our hearts.
Be a child within us
and then grow to full stature.

Come and be seen in us
*All* for the world needs your light.

*Leader* Lord Jesus Christ,
let the flame of your love
grow stronger within us
so that people will see,
not just a lantern
in the dark,
but a ray of the sun
which leads back
to the source of light.

Come and be seen in us
*All* for the world needs your light.

*Leader* Lord Jesus Christ,
come and be seen in us
this Christmas.
Make us lights
which show others
that there *is* a path
through the darkncss
– and that it leads to you.

Come and be seen in us
*All* for the world needs your light.

## *Star in the night*

*Leader* Lord, when you were born
in Bethlehem
there were armed soldiers
patrolling the streets
and distrust, bitterness
and conflict.

But there came
a star in the night
to lighten the darkness
and because the wise men were ready
to receive its message,
it led them to find you,
a baby in a manger.

We want to be ready to receive your message.
*All* Help us to find you this Christmas.

*Leader* Today, Lord,
in Bethlehem
there are still armed soldiers
patrolling the streets
and distrust, bitterness
and conflict.

But each year
Christmas comes to us
like a star in the night
to lighten our darkness
and if we too are ready
to receive its message,
it still leads us to find you,
not just in Bethlehem
but wherever people truly seek you,
for you came to be the light
of the whole world.

We want to receive your message.
*All* Help us to find you this Christmas.

# *Just Christmas*

Just a girl
with an outlandish message,
just a relationship
strained to breaking point,
just two people
facing the betrayal of love
– just Christmas.

Just busy roads
and hotels overbooked,
just the pain
and the mess of childbirth,
just the cry of the newly born
– just Christmas.

Just low paid workers
doing long hours at night,
just stillness
and the stars shining in the cold,
just the uneducated
seeing visions
– just Christmas.

Just travellers
coming from the east,
just a quest
riddled with doubts,
just seeking
in loneliness of heart
– just Christmas.

Just soldiers
patrolling the streets,
just political unrest
and corruption in high places,
just the innocent
suffering under those in power
– just Christmas.

Just truth
in small fragments,
just heaven
in the ordinary,
just God,
ignored and unnoticed
– just Christmas.

# *What a way to have a baby!*

She travelled on a donkey,
at night they both slept rough.
In the last stage of pregnancy
a journey's really tough.
No car ride to the hospital,
no ante-natal care,
no hygienic labour ward –
germs simply everywhere!
Nowhere to go in labour,
nothing to help the pain,
not even a bed to lie on –
just straw where beasts had lain.
No modern central heating,
just the cold night air,
no curtains at the windows,
stone walls, cold and bare.
No white-coated doctors
with sterile clothes to wear,
just Joseph and some animals
and smelly stable air.
What a way to have a baby!
where are the cards and flowers?
Just shepherds to share their gladness
in the midnight hours.

**'Before she married Joseph**
**she was in the family way.**
**She said an angel told her . . .**
**What a thing to say!'**

But Mary had her baby
before the light of dawn.
This was how it happened,
how the son of God was born.

*The words in bold could be read by a separate reader to give dramatic effect.*

# Epiphany

## *Brighter than the moon*

Lord Jesus Christ,
you are brighter than the moon,
more powerful than the sun,
more beautiful than the stars
and stronger than the wind.

You are the life-giving water
that can make gardens
in the desert.

Take our frail lives
and fill them with yourself.

So that wherever we go
parched ground
will become moist,
flowers will unfold
and trees will bear fruit.

Then there will
be seen in us
your brightness,
your power,
your beauty
and your strength.

For in you are hidden
all the secrets of heaven's wisdom
and all its shining treasure.

# *Thoughts at New Year*

Lord, let my life
be offered up to you
as a scented rose.

Let the shades of colour
give joy to your seeing.

Let the invisible fragrance
give joy to your breathing.

Let the touch of the petals
give joy to your feeling.

Let all my being
be pleasing to you.

So gradually,
as I grow with the thorns,
I may begin to share
in your eternal beauty.

# *Dedication*

*Leader* Let our going be in thankfulness,
*All* and our coming be in the service of the kingdom of heaven.

*Leader* Let our sitting down be in peace,
*All* and our rising up be in obedience to our Father the King.

*Leader* Let our hearts be for loving, as he directs,
*All* and our minds be for use in the ways of righteousness.

*Leader* Let our voices be for gentleness,
*All* and our hearing for listening with understanding.

*Leader* Let our deciding be with joy in all that is holy,
*All* and our very breathing be in the love of God.

## *The candle and the flower*

Lord Jesus,
you are the light
of the world.

And without light
all shape, form and pattern
are shrouded in darkness.

Without light
there is no growth,
no abundance of living.

Without light
there is no colour
in endless variation.

For within you burns
all light and from you
blossoms all beauty.

So, Lord Jesus,
you are truly the light
of the world.

But in your light
dwells all the beauty
of the world also.

# *And when it's all over . . .*

Baby Jesus, goodbye,
baby Jesus, goodbye!
We've put him away with the Christmas tree,
get him out again next year, maybe,
baby Jesus, goodbye!

**But Jesus grew to a man,**
**Jesus grew to a man.**
**He lived and he loved us so much that he died,**
**that is why God was crucified,**
**Jesus grew to a man.**

Baby Jesus is dead,
baby Jesus is dead.
In fact he was never there at all,
just a plastic doll in a cattle stall,
baby Jesus is dead.

**But Jesus rose again,**
**Jesus rose again.**
**He's alive and he cares about you,**
**he wants you to have eternal life too,**
**Jesus rose again.**

Baby Jesus is gone,
baby Jesus is gone.
He goes away with the Christmas cheer,
and then it's all over – till next year,
baby Jesus is gone.

**But Jesus is coming as King,**
**Jesus is coming as King.**
**He waits for you to invite him in,**
**he wants so much your love to win,**
**Jesus is coming as King.**

Baby Jesus, goodbye,
   baby Jesus, goodbye!
He's only a part of Christmas day,
   he'll not bother us – he's packed away!
Baby Jesus, goodbye!

*The words in bold could be read by a separate reader to give dramatic effect.*

# Ash Wednesday

## *From the wilderness*

*Leader* This is a dry and pitiless land
for here no flowers blossom
or birds sing,
there are no trees
to give shelter
from the sun
or grass to clothe
the rocks with green.

Lord, you are our only hope.
*All* We cling to you, do not forsake us.

*Leader* There is no gentleness
in the wind
or joy from the laughter
of children.
The dawn brings no hope
and the evening no comfort.

Lord, you are our only hope.
*All* We cling to you, do not forsake us.

*Leader* All those that love me
seem a long way off,
my heart is numb with sorrow
and my eyes are heavy with weeping.
I stumble trying to find
the right path.

Lord, you are our only hope.
*All* We cling to you, do not forsake us.

*Leader* I am like a dried-up plant
and my life – as meaningless
as dust blown by the wind.
Lord lift me out
of this deep ravine
for I am as helpless
as a little child.

Lord, you are our only hope.
*All* We cling to you, do not forsake us.

*Leader* Unless you rescue me
I shall be forgotten
and lost for ever.
Let me find your footprints
and be able to follow them.
for you also walked this wilderness
alone and forgotten,
and you are the only one
who can guide me through.

Lord, you are our only hope.
*All* We cling to you, do not forsake us.

# Mothering Sunday
## *Touch of love*

*Leader* Snowdrops and catkins are almost over
and crocuses grow gold, purple and white.
Bluebell leaves are showing
and the yellow coltsfoot smiles up at the sky.

Winter is over, the world has been reborn:
*All* at the touch of your love it's young once again.

*Leader* Buds on the trees are swelling
and daffodils are almost in bloom.
Birds flash their spring colours
and lambs can be seen in the fields.

Winter is over, the world has been reborn:
*All* at the touch of your love it's young once again.

*Leader* The sun sparkles on the water
and warms the river bank.
Old branches send forth new shoots
and flowers blossom on the bare earth.

Winter is over, the world has been reborn:
*All* at the touch of your love it's young once again.

*Leader* Everything is full of new life
and the promise of beauty to come.
It's your world, Lord, and you made it
and all the birds are singing for joy.

Winter is over, the world has been reborn:
*All* at the touch of your love it's young once again.

# *Lord Jesus, be welcome in our homes*

Lord Jesus, be welcome in our homes
and dwell in them.

Be a permanent member of our families
and know all our secrets.

Sit with us at every meal
and have your own chair by the fire.

Have your own place and possessions
and your own interests along with ours.

Be at every conversation,
as you listen to us, may we listen to you.

Have a part in all our plans
and a voice in all our decisions.

Be there at every argument
and when the air is heavy with tension.

Be in all our laughter
and in every whispering of love.

Share our sorrows as well as our joys,
our good days as well as our bad days.

As we open ourselves to you,
may you open yourself to us.

Let your beauty, love and peace
be found among us –

Lord Jesus, be not just a guest
in our homes but live in them always.

# Lent

## *How can I live without your beauty?*

I called to you, my beloved,
  but you did not come to me.
I searched for you
  but I could not find you.
There is no one else
  that can take your place –
  how can I live
  without your beauty?

For the strength of the winds
  is in your hands
  and the stars make a crown
  about your head,
  the majesty of moonlight
  weaves a garment for you
  and the desert becomes
  a garden where you tread.

Lord God, I have no right
  to command your presence
  or to be angry because
  you did not come to me.
But come to me, I beseech you,
  for I long for you with pain
  that breaks my heart.

Refresh my soul
  with your love
  and come to me –

  at the time
  of your own choosing.

# *Humility*

Humility
is like the snowdrops
flowering along the bank,
for they are
small and white
and they bloom in purity
low down
near the earth.

Humility
is like the goldfinch
perched in the tree,
for though he is
coloured with joy
in red, yellow,
black and white,
he cannot see
his own glory.

Humility
is like the seagull
soaring in the sky,
for his wings
are spread
in strength
with an easy grace
of which he is
totally unaware.

Humility
is like the buds
opening in spring,
for their
leaves unfold
with gladness,
responding
instinctively to
the warmth of love.

Humility
  is like the violet
  growing in the grass,
  for its birth
  is imperceptible
  and yet it is
  touched by God
  in the beauty
  of its growing.

# Holy Week

## *Loving leaves scars*

Is it not better
to be wounded
by caring too much,
than to become hard
by caring too little?

Loving leaves scars.

Some may be embarrassed by
those who are scarred
because they love
so deeply and so painfully.

They may say it was
their own fault
for getting involved,
not realising that
we all need help
to channel our caring
in the wisest ways.

Scars are not pretty things.

They may pride themselves
on their self-control.
They may shut their minds
to the suffering of others
that they cannot understand.

But Christ bears the scars
of his love for us all
in his hands, his feet and his side –

Does your love for others
leave scars upon you?

# *The choice*

Bread of God
broken for us,
wine of God
crushed for us;

Grain ground down
to give us food,
grapes destroyed
to give us drink,

each dying
to become
something greater.

Lord, you gave us
the pattern of life
in this bread
and this wine,
the ancient message
that is quickly
forgotten by
every generation;
the law of love
that was laid down
before the foundation
of the world,

that there is
no gaining
without losing,
no joy
without pain,
no singing
without sadness,
no light
without darkness,
no living
without dying.

For without breaking
the bread will be
locked in the grain,
without crushing
the wine will
stay in the grapes,
each of us
must die to become
something greater.

Bread of God
broken for us,
wine of God
crushed for us

you gave us
the pattern,
you came to show
us the way

– but the choice
is ours.

# *Betrayed*

What did you think about Judas, Lord?
I know you loved him,
  but you didn't stop him.

You would have forgiven him,
  of course you would.

But he killed himself
  and died unforgiven.

How could you live
  with that knowledge?
For three whole years
  he was one of your inner circle.

You saw him almost every day.
Did you know, all that time,
  even when you chose him
  to be one of your disciples,
  that he was going to betray you?

If you did know,
  I don't know how you could
  carry such a burden.

What did you feel
  when you told him
  that you knew
  what he was going to do?

Did you want to stop him, Lord?
Even after he'd betrayed you,
  did you want to call out
  after him, 'It's not too late
  to be forgiven'?

Lord, what did you think about Judas,
what were your feelings
and how did you cope with them,
when you saw him
walk out into the night
to his own destruction?

*The verses could be divided up between several questioning voices.*

# *The shadow of his sorrow*

The shadow of his sorrow
spreads across the city,
the shadow of his sorrow
covers humankind.
And his arms, outstretched,
touch the past and future,
the agony of everyone
erupts into his mind.

The shadow of his sorrow
covers every country,
there is no place or person
his shadow cannot reach.
He stands alongside all of us,
is one with all our crying,
he knows every kind of pain,
all that life can teach.

The shadow of his sorrow
steals around the universe
till natural light is darkened
and the sun must hide its face;
till that lonely figure
is the focus of all darkness,
and even heaven turns
its back upon the place.

'My God, my God, oh leave me not,
the darkness is intense.
The weight of sin upon my soul,
it shatters every sense.
My mind, it will disintegrate,
my heart is cold as death;
And my body, it is shaking
with every anguished breath.'

od, my God, where are you now?
y must I be alone?
W. . no pleading cry of mine
ever reach your throne?
The pain of all the universe
and none else to take my place?
And even you, my Father,
in sorrow hide your face!'

'It is finished! It is finished!'
The cry goes up to heaven.
'It is finished! It is finished!'
Now all can be forgiven.
I have carried all their sorrow,
I have carried all their shame,
I have carried all their darkness
within one human frame.

And the shadow of his glory
pierces through the universe,
the shadow of his glory
makes creation split in two.
For from his total darkness
springs up life eternal,
from the anguish of his dying
arises life anew.

# Easter

## *Risen Lord*

*Leader* You who transformed the world in your rising,
giving it new light,

*All* Risen Lord, we praise you.

*Leader* You who broke down the barriers,
going beyond the things we thought we knew,
destroying our illusions of the dark,

*All* Risen Lord, we praise you.

*Leader* You who changed the course of the river of life
so that its waters flowed across the edge of heaven and
into time,

*All* Risen Lord, we praise you.

*Leader* You who stretched our minds to take us out beyond
ourselves,
our safe assumptions and our own proud reasonings,

*All* Risen Lord, we praise you.

*Leader* You who shattered all our dreams –
to bring us to a more beautiful reality,

*All* Risen Lord, we praise you.

*Leader* You who lift us up so that we can be with you in glory
to see all things from where you are,

*All* Risen Lord, we praise you.

*Leader* You who scatter our small darkness
that we may reflect your radiance as from lesser stars,

*All* Risen Lord, we praise you.

*Leader* You who shine upon our beings here in time and in eternity –
light beloved and most glorious

*All* Risen Lord, we praise you.

# Ascension
## *The Prince of Light*

The angels crowded round him,
their faces shining bright.
The air was filled with music
to greet the Prince of Light.

Heaven was full of laughter,
its beauty all unmarred –
when suddenly a voice rang out,
'Look, his hands are scarred!'

A hush spread through the multitude,
and heaven held its breath,
for he who left an empty grave
still held the marks of death.

'I brought my scars to heaven
on hands and feet and head
so it will not be forgotten
I once was truly dead.'

'These scars are cruel and ugly,
yet here in heaven they stand.
Where all is light and beauty –
see now my wounded hand.'

'To you they mar my glory,
my wounds so raw and red' –
the hosts looked on in wonder
and many tears were shed.

'They are my greatest glory,
not things to make you sad.
These are treasured wounds,
rejoice and sing – be glad!'

'They are the price of love,
the reason why I died.
For I chose,' his voice rang out,
'*chose* to be crucified!'

# PENTECOST

## *Lead us in a plain path*

*Leader* Holy Spirit of God,
we need you so much
our minds are troubled
about many things.

Light up our minds
as the moon lights up the sky.
*All* And lead us in a plain path.

*Leader* We don't know what to do
and there is no one we can
ask for help but you.

Light up our minds
as the moon lights up the sky.
*All* And lead us in a plain path.

*Leader* Without you
all that is real within us
will shrivel up
and die away.

Light up our minds
as the moon lights up the sky.
*All* And lead us in a plain path.

*Leader* Come to us in the gentle
caress of the wind
and speak to us
in the tender shining
of the summer stars.

Light up our minds
as the moon lights up the sky.
*All* And lead us in a plain path.

*Leader* So Holy Spirit of God,
come to us and satisfy
our inward beings
with your beauty.

Light up our minds
as the moon lights up the sky.

*All* And lead us in a plain path.

# *The power of the Spirit*

Who can stand the wind,
  the wind of the Spirit?
No cosmic force
  can his strength withstand.
For with one breath of God
  the vastness of infinity
  rolls up like a plaything
  and drops into his hand.

Who can stand the fire,
  the fire of the Spirit,
  the lightning of God
  striking us within?
Pure joy of heaven,
  burning through our darkness,
  white fire of God,
  a holocaust for sin.

Who can stand the healing,
  the healing of the Spirit?
Who will ask for wholeness
  if it means his fire within?
Bowing to his power,
  acknowledging his greatness,
  letting in the light
  to cauterise our sin?

Do you want a part
  just a part of the Spirit?
Can we say to God,
'We'll have the joy and peace
  but keep the wind and fire –
  why, they might consume us!
Don't disturb our comfort,
  tell the storm to cease!'

Do you want the glory,
the glory of the Spirit,
the pure and brilliant beauty
that's cleansed and free from sin?
Then yield yourself to burning,
to blasting and to breaking,
for through these storms alone
comes gloriousness within.

So do you want the whole,
the whole of the Spirit?
We must have him in completeness
or we have him not at all!
For he is fully God,
he cannot be divided –
are you sure you want to risk
answering his call?

# *Do not underestimate the wind*

How the wind blows!
sweeping the grass,
tossing the trees,
hurrying from nowhere to nowhere;
turning, twisting,
and then returning
in a flurry of nothingness;
movements without purpose
and without pattern.

And yet the wind roars
and can ravage the defenceless earth.
Trees are torn up,
buildings destroyed,
floods let loose, and people can be tossed
like matchsticks into the air.

Do not underestimate the wind.

So is the Holy Spirit of God,
sweeping unseen across
the uplifted faces of the nations;
moving in ways
beyond our understanding.
Who would not smile
at children trying to catch
the wind in their hands?
Yet we try to confine him
in flurries of words
that disperse
into nothingness.

But he is the all-powerful God,
  surging through history,
  piercing dark clouds
  of sin, ignorance and fear.
He tosses aside the strong and wise
  like fallen leaves,
  and lifts up the weak,
  the foolish and the lost.
He blew across the void
  before time was,
  and will again
  when time is no more.

Do not underestimate the Holy Spirit of God.

# Harvest
## *The world is full of your beauty*

*Leader* Lord, you are King
*All* and the world is full of your beauty.

*Leader* The leaves are turning
russet and gold on the trees
and the hedgerows
are scarlet with berries.
Acorns and hazelnuts
hide in the branches
and brown satin chestnuts
burst from their cases.

Lord, you are King
*All* and the world is full of your beauty.

*Leader* Elderberries hang
in dark velvet clusters
and blackberries glisten
like jewels against
the blue of the sky.
The early mist hangs
a million crystal lamps
among the leaves to be lit
by the morning sun.

Lord, you are King
*All* and the world is full of your beauty.

*Leader* The corn is now
long harvested
and the fields are clad
in fertile robes
of furrowed brown.
The birds feed
on the autumn bounty
and swallows gather,
suddenly restless
with the call
of the far country.

Lord, you are King
*All* and the world is full of your beauty.

*Leader* Lord, I rejoice
in the knowledge
of your presence,
for you hold out your hands
to us in the beauty
of the world.
You touch us with
gentleness in the breeze
and your love enfolds us
in the sunlight.

Lord, you are King
*All* and the world is full of your beauty.

*Leader* The fruitful earth
laughs for joy
and sings in gladness
and we too will praise you
for the glory of your love.

Lord, you are King
*All* and the world is full of your beauty.

# *Lord God, King of the universe*

*Leader* Lord God, King of the universe,
*All* how great you are, how wonderful are all your works!

*Leader* Thunder and lightning flash from your throne
*All* and all the children of earth tremble at your presence.

*Leader* The rulers of the nations bow before you
*All* and all their power and might wither as plants in the desert without rain.

*Leader* How strong are your hands as you fashion the clouds
*All* and the mountains that rise up in praise to the holiness of your name!

*Leader* And yet your hands are gentle enough
*All* to make the smallest flower petal that drifts away on the summer wind.

*Leader* The beauty of your mind makes rainbows in the sky
*All* and clothes the world in infinite colour.

*Leader* Your love for each one of us
*All* makes us worthy of life and gives us dignity and honour.

*Leader* Lord God, King of the universe,
*All* how great you are, how wonderful are all your works!

# Remembrance Sunday

## *Playing with fireworks*

God, what are we doing to ourselves?
What have we unleashed?
Those in power are quick
   to tell us all is well –
   but I find no peace
   in their assurances.

For it is this very confidence
   that I find most disturbing.
For those who think
   they know the answers,
   or will have them very shortly,
   will not feel the need
   to come to you for wisdom.

God, we think we know so much,
   that there is nothing we can't handle.
But how much do we really know?
We have only scratched
   the surface of your knowledge.
We are as little children
   playing with fireworks
who think they have no need
   of adult supervision.

We have no time for you, God,
no time for you any more.
The human race has decided
   it has no need of you.

It is this arrogance
   that makes me tremble with fear
   more than the 'fireworks'
   we now hold in our hands.

For it is not these,
   it is our pride
   that is capable
   of blowing up the world.

# *Love must go on*

*Leader* There will be wars
and rumours of wars.
But God says,
'Do not be afraid,
for this is how
it has been
since the beginning,
this is not
a new thing
that is happening.'

Lord, give us courage
*All* and help us to love in the face of darkness.

*Leader* If we stop doing
the tasks God
has asked of us
or turn aside
from the paths
he has given us
to follow,
the darkness will win.

Lord, give us courage
*All* and help us to love in the face of darkness.

*Leader* It is more important
to love than it is
to be afraid.
Fear scatters love
and opens up
the darkness.

Lord, give us courage
*All* and help us to love in the face of darkness.

*Leader* God's love is what
the world needs.
It is easier to fear
than it is to love
but his love going out
through us is necessary
for the healing
of the world.

Lord, give us courage
*All* **and help us to love in the face of darkness.**

*Leader* There will be wars
and rumours of wars.
But God says,
'I am there with you
in the darkness
and beyond it
– do not be afraid.'

Lord, give us courage
*All* **and help us to love in the face of darkness.**

# *A name on a stone*

Private Davies –
was he young or old?
Was he dark or fair.
was he shy or bold?
Did he have friends,
kids and a wife?
How long did he have
to live out his life?
When the news came
that he was dead –
who was waiting
what tears were shed?
Those who remembered,
how long did they last?
Did memories fade
as years slipped past,
till just a brown photo
up on the wall,
was all they remembered,
remembered at all?

Private Davies –
how cold and alone
his name looks now,
cut in the stone.

And as I looked
I felt how sad
for those who thought
this was all we had –
just this life now,
like a candle flame
snuffed out for ever
when the end came.

How dark, how lonely,
with loved ones gone,
if we do not believe
that life goes on –
on beyond death,
a most thrilling thing
that is true and real
and makes the heart sing.
It makes living now
exciting and new,
that gives us purpose
in all that we do.
For with God even death
is not faced alone –

And no one ends
just a name on a stone.

# *Remembrance Sunday at the War Memorial*

**Child**

What are we supposed to remember today,
with flags and poppies and bands that play?
It's hard to keep still – two minutes is long!
but I just can't believe that anything's wrong.

**Young Woman**

I came here today as I always do.
I go to church every Sunday too.
I feel it might help violence to cease
if more came along and prayed for peace.

**Elderly Man**

I come here each year to keep faith with the dead,
the comrades I knew, like Billy and Ted.
They never grow old, those left were few,
I vowed I'd remember – what more can I do?

**Teenage Bystander**

I don't wear a poppy, as you can see.
Why should I bother? War doesn't touch me.
When everyone's dead it seems a bit late
to *now* be remembering – it's all out of date!

**Elderly Woman**

I came here to remember the man that I wed –
only three weeks after came the news he was dead.
Then my heart broke, now it's weary and sad,
mourning for children I never had.

**Young Boy**

I came here because I play in the band.
I like marching along, it makes me feel grand!
I've got tanks and soldiers, each with a gun,
  I like playing wars – I think it is fun!

**Bystander**

Why should I pray? Where's God to be found,
  when both my brothers lie under the ground?
Our street was wiped out, I saw it with tears,
  and loneliness, bitterness grow with the years.

**Child**

What are we supposed to remember today,
  with flags and poppies and bands that play?
It's hard to keep still – two minutes is long!
  but I just can't believe that anything's wrong.

# ALL SAINTS
## *People of faith*

I walked in the evening stillness
and I saw wheat standing
at the edges of fields
already harvested,
and I remembered Ruth,
gleaning in the fields of Boaz –

and I reached out
and touched her hand.

I walked in the evening stillness
and I heard a breath of wind
whispering in the trees,
and I remembered Nicodemus
coming to Jesus by night
and how Jesus turned
to the wind and said,
'So is everyone
that is born of the Spirit' –

and I bent my head
to catch the sound of his voice.

I walked in the evening stillness
and I saw clouds in the sky,
so many shapes and colours,
and I remembered Elijah
praying on Mount Carmel
and the little cloud
that arose out of the sea
no bigger than a man's hand –

and I stood beside him
gazing over the waters.

I walked in the evening stillness
and I remembered that we are surrounded
by a great cloud of witnesses,
a multitude that no man can number,
people of faith from every generation,
and as I reached out my hands to them,
I did not feel alone any more.

Today I walked in the evening stillness
and was comforted by God.

# *Endings and beginnings*

In you, Lord, there are no endings, only beginnings. Many times in my life I have felt I have come to the end but I did not understand then that you surround all things. Sometimes it feels as if I am dropping into an abyss but the abyss itself is in your hands and even death, the most final ending of all, will become a new beginning.

I can never move outside you, I can never go beyond you. You are the heartbeat of the universe and you are alive for ever. While you live nothing can truly be the end. You are the Alpha and the Omega, the beginning and the end. In you, Lord, there are no endings, only beginnings.

# *We can trust you as our guide*

*Leader* Lead us into the glory
of your love, oh Lord,
let us not falter
in our pilgrimage.
For the further beauty of love
is found beyond the horizon,
it is blended into more colours
than it is possible to comprehend.

We can trust you as our guide
*All* for you have trodden the way before us.

*Leader* But the greater glory of love
is found in the stumbling
along the path.
For the pain of the pilgrimage
is necessary to the arriving
and without it the journey
cannot be completed.

We can trust you as our guide
*All* for you have trodden the way before us.

*Leader* There are no short cuts or easy byways,
and the blood from the wounds
of you the crucified one
is found on the stones of the path.
But you will meet us at every turn
and refresh us on our journey,
for you are not only our goal
but the path by which we travel.

We can trust you as our guide
*All* for you have trodden the way before us.

*Leader* You bring heaven down to meet us
so we can recognise the landmarks
of our homecoming.
You are great and robed in majesty –
but still bear the marks of suffering
from your own pilgrimage.

We can trust you as our guide
*All* for you have trodden the way before us.

*Leader* Help us to be glad in your glory
amid the pain of our travelling.
For it will become ours also
as we follow in your footsteps.

We can trust you as our guide
*All* for you have trodden the way before us.

# *Homecoming*

White violets – in the snow!
in a place I do not know
and yet – it is familiar,

where summer roses grow
and autumn breezes blow,
all within one boundary,

where each beauty is apart,
yet mingled in its heart
in a single melody.

How can these things be?
– a sacred mystery
beyond my understanding.

For this place I do not know,
as new as pristine snow
without one footprint there,

is full of coming home
and the country is my own
and here I know belonging.